THE REPUBLIC of TED

Eddie Gibbons

THIRSTY BOOKS : EDINBURGH

First published 2003

Thirsty Books
is an imprint of
Argyll Publishing
Glendaruel
Argyll PA22 3AE
Scotland
www.skoobe.biz

British Library Cataloguing-in-Publication Data.
A catalogue record for this book is available from the British Library.

ISBN 1 902831 65 9

Beer/Soup
Ashleigh Ovenstone, The Pillars Bar, Dundee

Origination
Cordfall Ltd, Glasgow

Printing
Bell & Bain Ltd, Glasgow

To

Robert, Rita, Yvonne, and their families.

And to the memory of Peggy and Ted.

ACKNOWLEDGEMENTS

Thanks to Gerard Rochford for his astute comments on the text of *The Republic of Ted* section of this book.

To Elaine and Neil, Helen, the staff and many friends of the Bow Bar, Edinburgh for constant hospitality and hilarity.

To Eric, Jo, Christoph, Liz and Martin in Didsbury.
And to Barbara, Jenni and Alex, as ever.

Belated thanks to John Smith at Aberdeen Central Library for help and support over many years.

Special thanks to the Nursing Staff, wards A1, A3 & A4, Halton General Hospital, Runcorn, for their care of Ted during his final weeks.

CONTENTS

I ONE PURE NOTE

Transmission Lines 9

My Boss, The Sea 10

Machinery's Handbook 11

Lunch with Frank O' Hara 13

Volume to Weight 14

Frames 15

Why Buses Come in Threes 16

Requiem Bukowski 17

Shopping Forecast 19

Schrödinger's Cat Flap 21

Lovesick Nicorettes 22

Como 23

High Days, Edinburgh 24

II THE REPUBLIC OF TED

III LOOK AWAY NOW

Pageant 49

The Pain Equation 51

Syllabus 52

Confession 53

Resolve 55

Serial 56

Empty Now Grows Every Bed 57

Dressing the Table 58

What's This One Called Again? 59

Umpire of the Senses 60

Extract 61

Look Away Now 62

I

ONE PURE NOTE

TRANSMISSION LINES

My father built these rooms of love
with the strength of his own hands.
He daily made each sacrifice
protective fatherhood demands.

Monotonous compelling need
drove this toil of obligation.
Through the oil of grim machines
coursed the stream of his provision.

He marched among the factory crowds
throughout the sameness of his days:
clocking on and clocking off,
he laboured for a weekly wage.

His hands were grimed, his skin was rough,
yet tender was his warm concern.
He whispered calm into my fright
when courage failed and fever burned.

His work was food upon our plates:
his laughter was our daily bread.
The common currency was care
in that Republic built by Ted.

MY BOSS, THE SEA

In the grey estates of Industry
all outlooks are bleak. Windows
seldom show more than the
factory opposite, a dirty apex
of corrugated misery. Often
the view is a blank brick wall.

But in this new job one of the
windows looks out on the sea.
It is a small rectangular
blessing, a keyhole full of
weather, sending reports of
seagulls, currents and clouds.

Now and then, when I look up
from the universal oblong of
Windows 98 I can sometimes
see a tiny red ship take an age
to traverse the length of the
window ledge.

When I turn back to my screen
my boss is usually at my shoulder
branding me a dreamer
who should pay more attention
to desktop icons and less to
maritime meanderings.

So I continue drawing details
on my screen. When the prints
are issued they will be sent
to the client, who will build
a huge red ship and send it
sailing, tiny past my window.

MACHINERY'S HANDBOOK

Screw
You fiddle for hours
trying to find one
when dropped,

curse when it
binds, gripped
by its own story.

Clockwise is its grasping
aspect, the mating
stance, it advances

by turning away,
retracts in a sinister
fashion.

And when you're done
you toss it into a tin:
a rusting ballerina,

forgetting that once
it pirouetted
for Archimedes.

Lathe
Leonardo imagined it
as a pole with a cord.
It was no oil painting:
this turner was rough
and ready for anything.

Refined with the times,
resisting ornateness, its

greatness was in the slow
lubricated screw; coarse
or fine, left or right handed,

with precision that would
make you gasp. Finesse
is the watchword: it is
the barber of steel,
the engine of centuries,
the beautiful brute:
tooled up,
centred,
driven.

Welding Rod
Michelangelo painted it
between the fingers
of Adam and God:
the vital spark; life's
essential excitation.

Here a welding rod
paints an electric arc
between a welder
and two sheets of steel.

This is no light
in the firmament,
no symbol of the bond
between God and Man.

This is the arc
of the covenant
between poem and subject:
a small act of bonding
art and artefact.

LUNCH WITH FRANK O'HARA

I'm reading Frank O'Hara's *Lunch Poems*
during my break. I'm amazed
that Frank had a book by that title,
since that's when I mostly write.

I'm reading poems about his lunchtimes
in New York City, 1950s
The book is a cinema of words:
a Manhattan matinee.

Frank had two charms in his pocket
and a broken watchstrap on his wrist.
He died poetically on Fire Island,
hit by a dune buggy whilst carrying
his last poem in a gym bag.

Now, having shirked my writing
for the pleasure of reading
about a shoeshine in 1959,
I walk back to work
with a charming book in my pocket;
my watchstrap hanging by a thread,
my latest poem in my lunch bag.

VOLUME TO WEIGHT

The publisher said
my book of poems
would have broad appeal.

So I shed a few pounds
worth at readings
in pubs, libraries
and jazz clubs.

The audiences were thin
on the ground: an old man
and his dog, both deaf, and
the requisite drunken heckler.

I was getting fed
up with my meagre diet:
half-baked accolades
from half-pissed acolytes.

So I took my Slim
Volume to Weight
Watchers because
I thought it deserved
a wider audience.

FRAMES

He met her
at the Art Gallery.
Made eyes at her
across a Caravaggio.
Saw her framed
against a Miro.
Watched her glide along
an avenue of Monets.

She saw him standing
like a prick
between two Pollocks.

WHY BUSES COME IN THREES

The first bus leaves the depot on time,
picks up all the passengers
and drops them all off.

The second bus leaves the depot on time,
but now has fewer passengers to pick up
and so catches up with the first bus.

The third bus leaves from no depot.
It has no driver.
It glows a venomous green
and is made of pure spite.

REQUIEM BUKOWSKI

Hank, you lecherous
old fart.
You with your trailer
trash heart,
beating us up
with broken bottle
prose and piss
poor poetry.

Scoundrel slouch,
plug ugly as an ingrown
toenail, it's not just
the blackbirds that are
rough today.

Making a living
out of depravity
isn't writing:
it's as exciting
as a fag end
in the gutter.

And what you did
to your women
(hooch-cheap hookers,
slag heap lookers)
is best left unsaid.

Was your shroud
a dirty sweat-

stained sheet,
as you lumbered
drunkenly
from dead beat
to simply
dead?

Let's face it,
one of us
had to go.

SHOPPING FORECAST

The Shopping Forecast issued by the Dole Office
at 1930 on Thursday 8th June.

There are warnings of Sales in Frasers,
Debenhams, Esslemont and Macintosh.

The general Shopping List at 1300:

Iceland, North Utsire, South Utsire.
10p off at Iceland, while stocks last.
Lurpak £1.06 decreasing 5 or 6p
by 1300 tomorrow.
North it's dearer, south it's dearer.

Faeroes, Cromarty Co-op
Fisherman's Friends reduced
to tears. Automatic Lighthouse
on the blink. 40 watt
lightbulbs sold out.

German Bite, Biscuit, Thin as Air.
Strudels, Hob Nobs, 5p off.
Peckish, becoming famished 1 or 2
Decreasing 3 or 4
dress sizes.
Gail, forced, ate.

Isle of Jura, Baileys, Rhum.
70p off 70cl.
Westerly, veering uncertainly.

Becoming paralitic after 6 or 7.
Occasional slurring.
Dribble.
Poorly later.

Viking, Forties, GSOH
Low, 100 miles south of Shetland.
WLTM Siren or Silkie
No mermaids.
Rising Northwesterly
in anticipation.

Hiking, Base Rate, Robber Bank.
Variable, becoming high.
Extortionate for a time. APR 20 or 30.
Mastercard and Visa low.
Hard rain. Overdraft increasing 100%
Poor.

That is the end of the Shopping Forecast.

SCHRÖDINGER'S CAT FLAP

The cat flap is closed.
Is the cat inside or outside?

The pessimist's answer:
The cat is inside, curled up on the rug.
The optimist's answer:
The cat is outside under a truck.

Schrodinger's answer:
The cat is both inside and outside
at the same time.

The poet's answer:
Who cares if
the cat is sat on the mat
or the cat is splat and flat?

The world is all imagining:
the rhyme's the thing.

LOVESICK NICORETTES

I meet my friends at tables
in bars around the town.
We empty out our pockets
and lay the contents down.

Several pull out love affairs,
others their afflictions.
We sift and sort, sniff and scratch
our various addictions.

I'm smoking chocolate Woodbines
in place of cigarettes.
Others tend their torn-out hearts
with Lovesick Nicorettes.

They place them on the tender
bruised and burning places:
spites and hurts they've nursed for years
are withering their faces.

We talk, we drink, we raise a smile.
we drink our dreams to death.
Drunk, we only mention grief
every second breath.

We pocket our belongings.
We stand and we depart,
filling up the ashtrays
with our dog-end hearts.

COMO

At nineteen I plunged
into the lake at Como:
wide-eyed in clear water.

Baptised, I broke
into light,
gulped the cool air.

The lake
was postcard blue,
calm as prayer.

Silence towered
mountain-high.

A churchbell chimed
the one pure note
of my life.

Listen,
can you hear?

HIGH DAYS, EDINBURGH

This is a city you have to climb:
It's steps and stairways all the way.

The wind's as brash as a pantomime:
it steals your scarf and breath away.

The buildings boast majestic curves,
with all their windows gleaming.

The town is brick and span and verve,
with all its Saltires streaming.

II

THE REPUBLIC OF TED

VERNACULAR :

What you notice first
about my father
is his spectacular
vernacular:

the way he rounds
his diphthongs is sound
as a pound. His diction is
guttural with a nasal twang.

That night he sang
'Please Release Me'
at the Labour Club
is karaoke folklore,
though at the time
he called it *doing a turn.*

He'll drop his aitches
at the drop of a hat,
knock his vowels stone
cold flat and build
a sentence with syllabic
slabs as thick as doorsteps
on a Toxteth terrace.

His accent is one third Irish,
one third English
and one third catarrh;
his speech sounds like
an untuned guitar.

It's hard to avoid his
adenoidal lingo
when he's ordering
bevvies down at the Bingo
or telling me jokes
whenever I phone.

His voice sounds like laughter.
His voice sounds like home.

CAMERA OBSCURA :
(A trip to Edinburgh)

Scaling four flights of stairs,
we stopped at each level
for my father to catch
his breath and rest
his tired *Edinburgh Legs*.

In time we caught up
with the others
and entered the darkroom
of the Camera Obscura.

We gathered, séance-like,
around the plinth
where a pinhole and mirrors
projected the view
from the top of the tower:

the Castle, where tourists
trod their tiny paths;
the City, where toytown traffic
inched its way down Princes Street.

Then Calton Hill, the Firth of Forth
and Arthur's Seat.

We watched, like Greek Gods
might have done from Olympus,
small lives in motion
beneath our fingers.

Is this what death is:
a trick of the light?

And later, past holograms,
mirrors, light's hocus pocus,
a pinhole camera rendered
my father's upside-down face:
the fear of his x-rays sharply in focus.

DON'T PHONE FROM WORK :

Don't dial nine
for an outside line
to ask the Ward Sister
if he's any better.

The only words
she will utter
are *prostate*, *cancer*
and *pneumonia.*

Then a quiet insistence
to scoop you hollow –
Fly down today,
don't wait for tomorrow.

Show your new face
to the office floor –
set in a grimace,
wild, bewildered, raw.

THE MAN IN THE SACK :

On Sunday mornings
you'd take me to the Pier Head
to see Punch punch Judy
and watch the ferries waltz
to Wallasey.

I'd gasp as waves
rocked the Floating Dock,
feel faint at the sight
of the drop
glimpsed between slats.

Crowds of men
in old-fashioned hats
formed a ring around
a man in a sack
shackled by chains.

He became a blind
Dervish, his straining
and grunting scaring
the life out of
dozens of kids.

He twisted and feinted,
grappled and swerved
as if wrestling a demon,
while we shouted
Come on, you can do it!

Fifty years later
I have to unravel
your twisted blankets
to free your tangled
catheter tube.

You're wrestling with
a different demon.
I stand helpless,
chanting lowly
Come on, you can do it!

REMEMBERING THE FISH :

Receiving a smile
of rare recognition,
I chatted about
my journey from Scotland.

His evening meal
arrived on a trolley –
fish and chips,
ice cream and jelly.

He fumbled with
his knife and fork,
so I cut up his fish,
fed him four mouthfuls
before he was finished.

I stayed for five hours
although he was sleeping,
fussed with his blankets,
adjusted his pillows,
steeped in the silence
between his breathings.

The following day,
astoundingly lucid,
he claimed he saw no-one
the previous evening.

I joked that I'd walked
from Aberdeen,

and he couldn't recall
I'd even been.

He chewed the thought over
for several minutes:

Oh, yes,
you're right –
I remember the fish.

THE DOMINO EFFECT :

One small thing
leans on another,

grows into something
no one can gather
from the first signs
often looked over,

like that blank tile
I placed on the day
we played our last
game together –

you the child,
I the father.

When your spots
added up
to double sixes

no magic or hexes
could place the dies
back in their boxes –

the ones, the twos,
in natural order

with no wild numbers

to bring such disorder
as the bastard cells
that riot inside you.

DIRE MORPHINE 1 :

I phoned the hospital.
The Ward Sister answered:

He's had a bad night
but he's comfortable now.

I'm thinking of flying down
again tomorrow.

Yes, you should do that,
but due to the drugs
he probably won't know
who you are.

Maybe not,
but I know who he is.

DIRE MORPHINE 2 :

I arrive unrecognised –
a stranger in his room

He's taken apart
his diamorphine machine,
severed the pulsing artery tube.

His hands are agitating –
he's pulling tissues
out of a box, as if expecting
to pluck out a rabbit.

He's trying to drink milk
from a cardboard potty.

His eyes stare beyond me:
his mind is fifty years younger,
his face is fifty years older.
His mouth is set in a scowl.

His hands are still working
on the transmission line,
assembling endless unseen cogs.

He kisses my sister on the cheek
and says my mother's name.

The room is full of ghosts.

He's vexed and I'm fucked
if I am going to stand for it,
so I get the nurse
to change his dosage.

He is calmer now, though
I am more distraught-

his hands had shown signs of life –
signs of unseen cogs at work.

DOUBLE ACT :

We've always been
peas in a pod, me and you.
I'm the Toshack to your Keegan,
the Rush to your Dalglish.

I see your smile
when I look in a mirror,
catch myself miming

all your gestures.

But one half of us
is now half of himself
and any day now
I'll be left on the bench,

adrift from the source
of a lifetime's laughter;
doomed to the role
of a solo performer –

St John without Hunt,
Owen without Fowler,
out on a limb –
the lost lone striker.

WHAT NOT TO BUY HIM :

His seventh week in hospital –
still no positive results,
we're hesitantly optimistic.

I'm alone with my father.
He leans towards me and whispers:

Rita was in the Consultant's room
for half an hour this morning.
What do you think they said to her:

Don't buy him any LPs?

A1, A3, A4 :

Standard sizes
I use every day
for printing drawings.

The area diminishes
as the number increases.

A1, A3, A4 –
the hospital wards
my father's been through,
his failing health

turning him
from portrait to landscape,

decreasing the borders
of the Republic of Ted –

Those flowers.
That vase.
This bed.

DANCE THE NIGHT AWAY :

Wearied by the bedside vigils,
we decided one night
to push the boat out –
to celebrate
instead of pre-mourn you.

We played your favourite
music, sang the old songs
and danced until
night became day,

while the boat of your bed
drifted slowly away.

BEYOND LANGUAGE :

The Angel of Death appeared
in a light blue shirt.
He was wearing glasses.
He had a clipboard in his hand
and a badge that read
Macmillan Nurse.

He sat down
and gave my father
his inside story
in a measured,
matter-of-fact way.

The Angel had kind eyes
and a calm voice,
and I realised

he was The Angel of Life
with a tough job to do.
When he'd finished he left
his calling card and offered
If there's anything. . .

My father turned to me and

MAN OF THE CLOTH :

His final morning
of consciousness –

the nurse came in
to salve his crusted tongue
with swabs soaked in alcohol.

The first was whisky,
which he sucked with relish.

The second was Pernod,
which made him smile.

The nurse called a colleague
to see the look of pleasure
on Ted's face.

She had a bedcloth
folded over her arm.

When the nurse asked Ted
if he wanted anything else,
he pointed to the bedcloth
and said: *Soak that!*

THE LAUGHING MAN :

Did I sit beside that bed
for hours on end,
watching the clock's
grim reckoning
and the light's slow fading
draw its shadows
down the curtains?

Was there a catheter, a drip,
water that could not be sipped?

Was that my own father there,
or nobody I ever knew?
Was that face my father's face,
those hands the ones I'd held?

Those vacant eyes,
that open mouth-
that was never him.

But where is he –

the laughing man
I used to know?

Where is the boy
he used to be?

The soldier of Trieste?

That upright man reduced to this?

A SINGLE DROP :

I took the top off
his eye-drop bottle,
washed it out
and filled it with water.

I placed a single drop
on his tongue.
It choked him.

His body was beyond
my caring

and I found myself
choking on that single
drop of love.

NIL-NIL BY MOUTH :

Palliative?
What does that mean?

It means he can't take food or fluids –
he'll choke on a crumb or a drop.
The drip's turned off.

That evening, his last before the coma,

we draped his blankets in Liverpool colours.

Holding his hand, me and my brother
watched with him our last match together –
Auxerre away in the UEFA.

It was goalless when he gestured
for the nurses to bring the toilet.

Robert and I went for a coffee.
The nurses brought that pointless potty –
nothing had passed through his mouth for days.

He was living inside a morphine haze –
his eyes were open while he slept
and a lifetime passed between each breath.

It was still nil-nil when we returned.
Nil by mouth. No last words.

AGM/DNR :

Present:
Self, siblings.

Absent:
Hope.

Subject:
Father

Business:
To decide whether attempts
should be made to resuscitate
the subject should the drugs
cause a heart attack.

Staff Nurse Pamela
provided tea and biscuits.

Death took the minutes.

SPEED BUMPS :

They're a curse!
said the ambulance driver
as we crested the seventh
tarmac wave and you winced.

I took your hand,
caressed your brow –

It's OK, we're nearly home.

The paramedic next to me
said they'd complained
endlessly to the council –

It's poor sick sods
like your Dad that suffer.

I nodded as we shunted
the last bump
and the motion made
you sigh one final time –

your breath rising
and falling
like wind over the ocean.

THE WEIGHT :

How far is it now, Ted?
Not far, Joe, not far, mate.

They're halfway between Woolfall Heath
and Broadgreen. Nightime, 1938,
halfway down a three-mile route;
Ted in his hand-down shoes,
Joseph in his scuffed-up boots.

They passed the Page Moss terminus
too late for any bus, too skint to hail
a cab. No ambulance in sight tonight –
Shanks's pony is the only way to go.

It hurts, Ted.
I know Joe, I know.

This is Joe's final journey, Ted's longest
trek. Joseph is on Ted's back, racked
by pneumonia. Joseph is twelve, Ted,
a year his junior. Joe is heavy, but
he's his brother.

At home, their fretting mother
ties knots in her rosary
for every pavement slab between
Woolfall Heath and Broadgreen.

AT DEATH'S DOOR :

He left the room
but the door was closed.
Where did he go?

Death took him.
You saw it.
You were there.

I saw nothing
that was not
there before.

But something changed. . .

Yes, I remember now:
I heard him breathing,
then I heard nothing.

Death is a silent thief.

I kissed his forehead.
It was cold.
Cold in minutes.

Death takes everything.

So Death caused his dying?

No, Life did that.
Dying is a lifetime's work.
Life closes the door.

And what does Death do?
Death slams it shut.

A PENNY FOR THE GUY :

Every bonfire night we'd pinch
your old shirts,
shoes and pants
to dress the Guy
for his moment
of fame,
then watch him
disappear
in flames.

Now you, too,
have gone out
in a blaze of glory.

We told the story
to the papers –

your *mori*,

our *memento* –

Small Ads:
Deaths;
received an invoice
from *The Echo*.

All you were,
all you did,
and a penny change
from fifteen quid.

WHAT HE WASN'T :

You're asleep, the notice said,
beyond this world's despair.

He wasn't sleeping, he was dead.
There is a difference there.

No angels sang around his head.
His head was cold and bare.

No Ship of the Soul, no Golden Thread.
Not one celestial trumpet blared.

What final words might he have said?
Peggy, are you there?

REUNION :

I'm handed the casket
containing your ashes.
It weighs the same
as I did as an infant.

Kneeling, I lower you
into the ground
where my mother was
buried nine years before,
completing this final
tender reunion.

Pressing gently,
I move you toward her,
as once you pressed gently
lover to lover,
producing the hands
that now tremble above you.

I stand to face
your gene congregation
and read the poem
that choked in my throat
at each rehearsal
for seven days passing
but now rings clear
as a church bell chiming.

All heads are bowed,
a last prayer is whispered;
we walk, diminished,
into the future.

THE DAY AFTER :

I looked out on Helsby Hill
each day above your windowsill.
I watched in shadow, rain and sleet;
morning, afternoon and night.

The day before your day of days
the hill stood in a drizzle haze.
And when the paramedics came
we took that last short journey home.

Today I'm here and you are gone,
on Helsby Hill I stand alone
and watch the clouds go drifting by
beneath the endless empty sky.

The day is fresh and bright and clear,
the hospital's just over there –
and now I wish I could contrive
to be back there, with you alive.

III

LOOK AWAY NOW

PAGEANT

The future yawns like a door
opening in a strange town.
You step through it.
You lay your suitcase down
and unpack your desires.

This is the town in your dreams.
Your hotel room looks onto
an unlit street, where you catch
a glimpse of the past, shuffling
its tawdry husk round a corner.

There are muffled cries from
the room next door. It is your
parents having endless orgasms.
You've never thought of them
this way before. You grab a razor

and shave the five o'clock
shadow from your six o'clock neck.
The clock itself is shamefaced and
hides behind its hands. You tick
it off for all the unkind years.

Room service arrives with invitations
from all your unrequited loves.
You enquire about the names
on the cards. You've never met these
people, but it seems they know you.

The noises from the next room
have stopped. The silence startles.
Your parents are buried
beneath a quilt, children again,
breathing clouds of forgetfulness.

It seems that the wallpaper
is newspaper from another planet.
Closer inspection renders it
as the story of your life in every
language but your own.

Your clothes belong to a stranger.
You see your image in the shoes.
So this is the future face into which
the more familiar one is growing?
Mirrors shatter all around.

Sounds surf through an open window.
Below is the pageant of your childhood:
figures hopscotch through rings of roses;
several fall and bleed while others chant.
A child is eating a bucket of ashes.

The bare bulb on the ceiling flickers
its dull morse. The wallpaper peels
to reveal a starry sky. This is the future:
your father and mother walk quietly
to their graves. They turn and wave.

THE PAIN EQUATION

I was late for school again,
even though I was riding
my brand-new
Carlton Vitesse bicycle
with Campagnolo gears.

At the school entrance
my satchel slipped
and jammed in the spokes.
I was the first kid ever
to arrive head-first
through the school gates.

I got up cut and bruised
to the solo applause
of a fellow straggler:
Fatty Hardcastle, who could
tell you the logarithm
of any number off the top
of his head.

It made no odds to him
that he was late for Maths as well:
he was A-Level material at twelve.
To his credit, he picked up my bike
and took me to the nurse.
Then he sauntered off to teach
the teacher a thing or two
about the Numbers Game.

Ever since that incident
I've equated numbers with pain.
I arrive headlong to appointments
with bankers and accountants,
bleeding and bruised, clutching
my spoke-shredded wallet.

SYLLABUS

Algebra came first
in the list of fears,
followed in later years
by the demon of calculus.

Learning by rote,
we were never taught
that independent thought
could turn a minus to a plus.

Or that our real exams
would mark us for life:
stress, tedium and strife
would be our syllabus.

CONFESSION

Forgive me, father, for I have rhymed
coat with boat and loving with longing.
Believe me when I say it was never
my intention to commit such crimes.
How things came to such a pretty
pass is hard to recount, my being from
stout working class stock – a son of toil,
a grain of earth salt. I was a red brick
and rain child with holy socks and grazed
knees. Please take into account the fact
that I once beat the shit out of Davy Graham
that night his gang jumped me behind the chippy.
He hit me first but I felt no pain. Adrenaline
is the one true drug. I shrugged when he fell
to the ground for the final time and I looked
around at faces etched with fear and respect.
I expect no clemency for writing poetry,
it's a heinous act, but consider the fact that
I lifted that tenner from the sweetshop counter
and went back later for the evening paper
and brassed-out the shopkeeper's dirty looks.
Did I spend it on books? Like fuck I did –
that ten quid bought a ticket for Inter in
the Kemlyn Road, three pints of bitter
in the Arkle pub and a ten bob sub to my brother
to pay the Tally and his fares to work.
I never shirk my duties where family's
concerned – every penny I earned went to mum,
dad and wife, and what I had left was a short-change
life which needed supplementing somehow, so I turned

to crime, petty not pretty. I kept my hand in
someone else's pockets. Learned the thrill
of a ransacked till, the pleasure in parting
the leather of a pilfered purse and rolling a wad
in my fevered mitt. It's a hit no drug can ever match:
like lifting the latch of a shut-up shop, sweeping
the ciggies into a sack then vaulting the wall
to the alley out back without alarming a dog
or a cat. Father, I know you'll forgive me
for that, but not my cackhanded knack
of pummelling prose into poem-sized pots.
Bring out your cross, your altar and mitre
and save this poor sinner from robbing the metre.

RESOLVE

As from today I will not walk slower
when someone approaches. It's a habit
from childhood, when pavements were
anxious places teeming with hardknocks
with angry faces. A walk to the shops
was a hazardous venture, with stone-
throwing snipers and gangs on each corner.

As from today I shall not falter
from making the tough incisive decision –
there'll be no division between will
and action; no hesitation, no crippling
distraction. I'll banish the dither, the
waver, the shiver and kick into touch
the moan and the bicker. No longer
the ball-boy. Now I'm the striker.

As from today I will not flinch from eye-
to-eye contact: I'll steel my nerves and
enter the contract of looker and looked-at
without so much as a wince or a squint,
and fix my gaze with steely intent on
whoever's pupils hook my attention.
No stare or glare will wither my will.
Fasten your buckle for a white knuckle
ride if you dare to look me in the eye.

SERIAL

I killed the boy with the bouncing ball,
his tousled hair was matted with blood.
The ball went bouncing down the street
and stopped in a gutter of mud.

I slayed the lad in his early teens,
wiped his smile with a barbed wire noose.
Smashed his records, slashed his shoes,
burnt cigarette holes in his suit.

I slashed the student with a knife,
felt the steel rip through his guts.
I carefully cut out his heart.
and filled the hole with ten pound notes.

Then I shot my wife's last lover,
served his balls up to the dog,
wrapped the corpse in a satin cover,
buried it in a grave of fog.

Ball, wire, knife, cover:
growing old can be murder.

EMPTY NOW GROWS EVERY BED

What once was done
is now undone.
What once was near
is far away.
And love that lighted
on your shoulder
in some distant June
or May, has lifted now
and flitted skyward,
out of vision,
flown away.

Who once was here
is now elsewhere.
The one who held
your sleeping head
now holds another's
in its slumbers
in some distant town
instead. Like hearts
and houses, cribs
and cradles, empty
now grows every bed.

DRESSING THE TABLE

Sitting in the pub,
drinking alone, he dresses
the table with empty glasses.

Into the humdrum bar,
its vagabond bands hunched
beneath a blether-stained ceiling,
glide two templates of loveliness.

They sit at the bar and glow
like a Higher State of the Flesh.
They exist to be adored.

One glances towards him,
thrilling a wave through his whisky.
The other follows suit,
turning his Tamnavulin tidal.

Seasick and lovesick, he ogles them
but receives no further recognition.

Then he turns to his whisky's
wavelength and is drowned:
he remembers the mirror behind him,
the true target of the girls' glances.

They depart to a fluttering
of ageing hearts, leaving
these lessons behind them:

they are immune to glances
from shop-soiled chancers
and they never mate
outside their species.

WHAT'S THIS ONE CALLED AGAIN?

They come more frequently now
than they did an hour ago:
those over-fifty moments
when you simply can't remember
what on earth (or perhaps elsewhere?)
you did over fifty moments ago
(sometimes less than that).

You've waved goodbye
to your memory
your sanity and your cat
(thinking it was your wife)
and as you open the
– big rectangular piece of wood
with a handle and a keyhole –
you wonder:
what's this brolly for?
Why am I wearing a hat?

All those things you knew by rote
have sailed away in a pee-green boat.

All the books are overdue
in the library of your mind.
There's something you used to know
regarding madeleines. . . (what?)
Is it because you've misplaced your
– small round objects the doctor gave you?

Remembrance of things has passed,
like the memory of an onion and
those blue forgotten hills.

UMPIRE OF THE SENSES

My sense of smell
was snipped
when a surgeon's
scalpel slipped.

I've smelt my last rat,
sniffed my last Bisto,
can't tell if I'm
in a bog or a bistro.

One fifth of me is dead –
my nose is only a hole in my head.
It seems my personal audio
will be the next to follow.

The sound of leather on willow
has faded to feather on pillow
and roaring racing cars
are wasps trapped in a jar.

The Umpire of the Senses
has declared a follow-on:
my eyeslight's gone all googly,
they've made me Nightwatchman.

Words that once were fixed in type
float like they've just fixed on coke –
I'm reading Alexander Poop
and *Infant Goy* by William Bloke.

EXTRACT

I want to leave this poem
under your pillow
(like the tooth fairy
leaves you sixpence
under your pillow)
to show you clearly
the true correlation
between writing
and pulling teeth.

LOOK AWAY NOW
(If you don't want to know the score)

The Linesman's flagging,
and so is your team.
A figure in black
is haunting your dreams.

He's judge and jury
of who is at fault.
The season will turn
on this one result.

The banners are sagging.
The chanting has stopped.
Your wife's disappeared
while out at the shops.

A note on the table,
a valediction,
a wedding ring pinned
to the inscription.

The girl from your office
has spilled the beans
to your wife on the phone,
a bitter scene.

Your daughter's in bed
with that prick next door.
He's brought all his Mates
to show her the score.